Just being here
By Richard K Page

Contents

ACT ONE

An evening street at night time. The stage is light partially on the left hand side. The light is coming from the local pub and chip shop. Just on the edge of the lighted stage a man enters. Dave Morley a stocky man of just above average height. He is in his late 30's early 40's. His head is shaven but not completely. He stands hesitantly on the edge of the shadow and the light.

DAVE: (to the audience) Nothing changes here. No matter how long you've been away. Same old crappy pub, smelly chippy. (to himself) What you doing Dave? Just keep walking…

There is the sound of a door opening. In the background, a busy pub crowd can be heard for a few seconds. Then the sound goes quiet as the door can be heard shutting. Enter Ollie onto the stage into the light. He is carrying a cigarette in his hand. He is swaying slightly. At first he is unaware of Dave. Then as he concentrates with limited success on getting the cigarette in his mouth, he becomes aware of Dave in the shadows.

OLLIE: Bloody hell. Who the Christ are you? Sir Lurkalot? Almost drop me fag.

Dave comes into the light but retains a reasonable distance from Ollie. Ollie is rummaging through his pockets as if trying to find something.

OLLIE: (to Dave) Got a light mate

DAVE: I don't smoke.

OLLIE: You do right mate, another bloody establishment conspiracy to keep the workers down. And then they make us stand out in the sodden cold.

Ollie stops mid rant and looks more closely at Dave.

OLLIE: Don't I know you?

DAVE: (unsure) No mate. New to the area.

OLLIE: Funny never forget a face. Still why don't you wait here? Brian in the Chippy always has a light for us. Then you can come buy me a pint. Seeing as you're new to the area.

Ollie staggers off and exits towards the Chip Shop.

DAVE: (to audience) Jesus that was close. Of course, I knew him Oliver Dunbar or plain Ollie or plain dumb if you ask me. I've chucked him out of every boozer in town centre the bleeding piss head. Mind that was a lifetime ago. Literally. Look I'm going to have to go. You're gonna hear things about me. Christ, I deserve some of them. But remember there but the grace of God. And don't be quick to judge. Why did I come here? I had a world I could have walked in, but I come back to this shit hole. What? To make amends to say sorry. To hope they'll understand. Come on Dave. You where lucky only Oliver Reeds twin brother saw you tonight. Anyone else and the locals would have been lighting their torches and sharpening their pitchforks.

Dave exits in a hurry. For a moment the stage is clear. Then Ollie comes staggering back. The cigarette now lit. He at first doesn't notice Dave has gone.

OLLIE: Good old Brian knew he'd sort me out. Mind you Madge had a face like a bulldog chewing a wasp. Now this pint.

Ollie notices Dave has gone.

OLLIE: Fucking weirdo. I know I know him from somewhere. No, it's not going to come out of the old computer tonight

Ollie taps his head and staggers to exit stage.

ACT ONE SCENE TWO — Chip Shop Counter.

Chip shop same evening, 10 pm, mid-May, Marge is focused on a customer while Brian is singing "Wooden Heart" in Pigeon German while shaking a chip basket.

Brian: (quietly to himself, sings) Mussy den, mussy den, vou shake-a-lady now, shake a lady now, un bits mine heart und den. (Humming the rest while Marge speaks)

Marge: Ten pounds going in (said aloud), that's three fifty and fifty makes four, a one makes five n' five your change love, thanks very much.

Customer1: Ta! (Walks out)

Marge: Can we have two more fish in please Brian, I'm all out.

Brian: Coming right up Marge me love, what's with you tonight, you're being very polite?

Marge: I've decided to better myself; the first step is the perception to those around me.

Brian: Perception eh! I've never been one for perception me, what you see is what you get.

Marge: Yeah! Bloody right, I tell you, what I perceived before we married is not what I bloody got.

Brian: Yeah, well you 'avn't changed one bit my little dumpling.

Marge: Don't you dumpling me?

Just then another customer walks in and both turn to face as the bell on the door rings and their conversation is interrupted.

Marge: Are you wanting chips love, were waiting on chips, they'll be 'bout 5 minutes.

Customer2: (long) mmmm, yeah, can you chuck me a fish without batter in too please.

Marge: And a fish without batter Brian. (Brian is well within hearing distance and shakes his head in mild annoyance) Anything else there love?

Customer2: No, no that's it, plenty of Salt n' vinegar though please.

Brian: New kebab machine coming next week my mate, you'll be able to get something a bit more spicy next week.

Marge: Since when?

Brian: (sings to the tune of Heartbreak Hotel) Since when my baby left me..., what do you mean since when?

Marge: (Marge rolls her eyes) Since when are we getting a new kebab machine?

Brian: Since I ordered one a fortnight ago, I'm sure I told you.

Marge: A fortnight ago, You didn't consult with me on this?, I'd have remembered if you if you told me, you don't tell me nothing, I swear, I swear you think I'm bloody Doris Stokes.

Brian: Since when do I need to consult with you?

Marge: Since I became your wife....AND! Business partner.

Brian: Aye a remember the wedding n' all, but I don't remember selling you any shares in the business.

Marge: You didn't have to sell me any shares; I adopted them when we married.

Customer2: She's got a point, what's yours is hers n' what's hers is her own n all.

Brian looks at the customers sternly, while Marge gives an appreciative nod.

Brian: No, you were an employee of the company when we met, when we married, and your still an employee of the company now, "never mix business and pleasure" that's my motto.

Marge: I don't remember any bloody pleasure as long as I've known you besides I'm your wife.

Brian: So!

Marge: I'm your wife, and it's your company, so I own 50% of the company. Plus I'm an employee so technically I'm more in charge of this chippy than you. So I think I should have a say in whether we get a bloody kebab thingy or not....especially since it'll be me bleeding cleaning it! And I'm having my say right now.

Brian: Perception Marge...customers in, remember Perception!!!

Marge scowls at Brian.

Marge: Two more minutes on them chips love. So, what's with the sudden Kebab thing then anyway?

Brian: I just thought it would provide a little more choice for the let out from Farmers.

Marge: You mean Ollie and his mates.

Brian: No, I mean customers in general; they're always asking if we do kebabs, especially when they kick out at the Farmers, "supply and demand" that's my motto.

Marge: What happened to "Business and Pleasure"? You're happy to combine business and pleasure when it comes to your mate's pleasure and our bloody business, kebab machine my arse. No! Only that bloody Ollie, n' his shower of shites, they're the only ones who asks for kebabs.

Brian: Perception!

Marge: (turns back to customer2) Sorry love

She starts to gather together the bags, and papers to assemble the food order.

Marge: Any news on that fish?

Brian: No we only use clean paper now, have done for about twenty years something to do with lead in the ink.

Marge: I'll put lead in you in a minute, I mean is it ready?

Brian: (still pleased at his last joke) No it's yellowy.

Marge: For God's sake! Sorry love, he's been in one of those moods all night.

Brian: Hey I'm on a roll....just like some chips eh, bread roll eh! (Elvis style) "Thank you very much".

Marge: So that's one fish without...., chips, plenty of salt an' vinegar, anything else my darling?

Customer2: No that's it, thanks.

Marge: (Sniffs) Them fish are burning,

Brian: No they're not

Marge: Well something's burning.

Brian: Only my love for you, sweetheart, only my love for you..(sings) I'm just a hunk a hunk of burning love, I'm just a hunk a hunk of burning love.

ACT ONE SCENE THREE — The Farmers Arms.

Inside the Farmers Arms, Colin and Ollie are sat at the table; they're on their second pint.

Ollie: That's where they have you see. It was exactly the same with the civil rights movement in America. They brought all those slaves across from Africa, to get them picking cotton and tending farms they had to house them, provide them with a health care of sorts, feed them, it was too much to administer.

Colin: Yes but they're free now.

Ollie: Are they bloody hell, neither are we. (beat) See they have us thinking it's all about money, it's not, money was only installed as a mechanism to control the masses. We're all still slaves in an ancient feudal system, black or white, we're all slaves.

Colin: How does that work?

Ollie: Well you see back when we peasants were slaves, it was up to our lord and master to feed us and to put a roof over our heads. This took time and effort, just like the landowners in America.

Colin: So?

Ollie: Well, obviously no one was happy to be slaves and so we had to be watched all the time, locked down and that took even more effort. Otherwise, we'd of skipped wouldn't we?

So then they thought, right we'll pretend to set them free, we'll still get them to work building our empire, but we'll give them shiny coins, the harder they work, the more shiny coins we give them.

Then we'll pretend, the elites that is, to lend them hundreds of shiny coins with which they can buy some land and a house, from us. Then they have to work another twenty five years, to pay back the money we invented and loaned them, to pay for the house the other slaves built that we used to have to give them for free.

Colin: I thought the banks lent us the money?

Ollie: Yeah, but they own the banks, the land and the companies you buy anything from, it's all one big corporate state owned by the elite. You look up any big company, it's owned by another unheard of company that owns all the other companies that you buy stuff from.

Colin: The rich?

Ollie: Yes, well no, I told you, money is only for us slaves, the elite don't need money, you've heard the saying "free to those that can afford it".

Colin: What about Brian, He owns his own business, so he has no master has he bucked the system?

Ollie: Ah! But he's the biggest slave of all, you see he's totally sold on the shiny coin notion and they have taxes to catch the likes of him. You see, despite working for himself he still contributes to the economic cycle, all his money comes from the other slaves rather than trickling down from the elite... and he had to buy two houses, one for living in and one for his chippy, don't forget they mint the coins for nothing, his chippy keeps the other slaves down. The only ones that really buck the system are those that to refuse to work for the system at all.

Colin: Right-right-right, like you then?

Ollie: Exactly, it's just my little stand against the corporate machine. I mean, who said it was their land in the first place aye?

Colin: So do they own the breweries as well then?

Ollie: Everything.

Colin: So you're helping them by drinking that pint!

Ollie: No I'm not.

Colin: But slaves had to work for the corporate AND pay taxes to pay your dole so you could buy that pint and that pints profit goes back to the corporate via the brewery who enslave all the brewery workers.

Ollie: hmmm your right, I never thought of that, tell you what, you'd better get the next one in, just to be on the safe side.

Janice, the barmaid comes to the table collecting glasses.

Janice: Are these dead now love?

Colin: Yep, cheers love.

Ollie: Janice, did you know you were a slave to the elite corporate machine.

Janice: No, I just thought I was a slave to fashion.

Colin: We're all slaves according to Ollie.

Janice: May as well be a bloody slave, though, I've been on since four, that cow Becky ain't turned up and it's me slimzone night tonight. I was only supposed to be here till eight.

Colin: Slimzone! What do you need to go slimzone for? There's nothing of you!

Janice Have you never watched "you are what you eat", its true, "YOU ARE WHAT YOU EAT!"

Ollie: So what have you had to eat tonight then?

Janice: Just a banana.

Ollie and Colin burst out laughing, Janice shakes her head at their childishness and walks away. Ollie & Colin admire her rear view. Turn and look at each other in approval.

Colin: I wouldn't mind having a slave like that.

Ollie: Aye, me n' all.

Colin: Do you think she'd be in to all that?

Ollie: Oh Aye, you can tell?

Colin: How?

Ollie: Women like that, see how she's always wearing very high heels and black stockings, she's one of those dominatrixes.

Colin: fuck off!

Ollie: She fucking is I'm telling you, I can just imagine her stood there, thigh length boots, suspenders, Basque and a whip, with me tied to the bed.

Colin: So no objections to being a slave there then?

Ollie: Ah well, sex slave that's a different matter.

Colin: Really!

Ollie: Damn right.

Colin: I didn't think you'd be into that.

Ollie: Bloody right I would.

Colin: Hmm interesting.

Ollie: Why.

Colin: Well you see by definition "a slave" is one who is forced to do things against their will for no reward or payment.

Ollie: Yeah.

Colin: Well, you see, since with Janice you'd be willing, you wouldn't really be her "slave" so to speak, you could only really be a sex "slave" if your master was someone you weren't so willing to be with…. Such as Dozy Dave over there.

Ollie: Fuck off!...Hold on (said with increasing speed on each Dave) Dave, Dave, Dave, Dave, Dave, Dave, Dave, Dave, Dave, Dave Dave, (quicker) Dave,Dave,Dave,Dave Dave (realization) Dave FUCKING MORELY..!!!

(Janice glimpses back from a distance in recognition).

Across at another table

Mavis: It's cold in here, are you cold in here? , I'm cold in here me.

Sal: No, I'm warm me, I'm always warm. If I was in an igloo, I reckon I'd be warm.

Mavis: Well I'm cold, there's a draft coming in from somewhere.

Carol: Ooh, I liked him!

Sal: Who?

Carol: Shaft.

Sal: Shaft, who mentioned Shaft?

Carol: Mavis!

Mavis: Who's Shaft, I've never bloody heard of him.

Carol: You said something about Shaft coming in from somewhere.

Mavis: No.. I said there's a draft coming in from somewhere, ooh god, you never listen do you, you never bloody listen you, she never listens.

Well, I don't bloody know Shaft, who the bloody hells Shaft anyway.

Sal: Oh you remember Shaft bloody big black man, was a policeman in the seventies, oh he was gorgeous.

Mavis: You didn't get black police men in the seventies, no not in the seventies. There were never any in the seventies, not black ones anyway.

Carol: He's not real!

Mavis: What he' wasn't really black?

Carol: No, he wasn't really a policeman, it was a bloody film.

Mavis: Ooooh! ey, you wouldn't…., with a black man would you? Would you?

Sal: Ah-bloody would, ooh aye you know what they say.

Carol: Well my Erik reckons that black or white, they're all pretty much the same size. A white man's well it starts off little but grows when they get all excited. Whereas your average black man's well it starts off big but stays the same size, it just gets firmer that's why it looks bigger when they're not excited.

Mavis: Ooh, is that why they call them Shaft?

Sal: No, they're not all called Shaft, just him, Shaft.

Mavis: Well I like that other one, such lovely eyes, oh and the smile. He had a lovely smile for a darkie didn't he, lovely smile.

Sal: Which one?

Mavis: Sidney Potter played that teacher. Please sir, from Russia with love.

Carol: Poitier, Sidney Poitier and it was "to Sir, with love."

Mavis: Close enough, Is he French then?

Carol: No he must be English, he taught English in that film, very well spoken

Mavis: Sounds French to me, don't you think Poitier sounds French?

Sal: Ooh, me and that Shaft, in an igloo.

Carol: What rubbing noses like what them Eskimos do?

Sal: Inuit's

Mavis: What?

Sal: Inuit's, we're not allowed to call them Eskimos anymore it's not politically correct.

Mavis: The blacks?

Sal: No Eskimo's, we now call them Inuit's.

Carol: I don't know any bloody Eskimos.

Mavis: I know what an Eskimo is!

Sal: So?

Mavis: Well I don't know what an 'inyourthingy' is? Do you, I don't.

Sal: It's an Eskimo!

Mavis: So why not just say Eskimo then?

Sal: Because it's not politically correct.

Mavis: Well it's not bloody politically correct to talk to me about something that I don't know what it is, I mean, I know what an Eskimo is. I've already said I know what an Eskimo is.

Sal: It's the same thing!

Mavis: Well I Know that now, but I didn't before, ooh I don't get why they have to keep changing the names of things, it's the same bloody thing!!!

Sal: Because it offends people.

Carol: But we don't know any Eskimos?

Sal: You never know, he could be an Eskimo there. (pointing to someone in the pub)

Carol: Is he bloody hell.

Sal: He could be, look, he's got a duffel coat on.

Mavis: I told you it was cold. Didn't I, I said all along its cold in here, and there he is a bloody Eskimo.

Carol: So what do they say about them Inuit's thingies then are they big?

Sal: Ooh I don't know, I reckon they'd be pretty small

Mavis: Why?

Sal: Because it's so bloody cold in them igloos. I wonder if that would affect Shaft. Oh, I would be disappointed.

Mavis: Well take him somewhere warm then.

Sal: Oh yeah, alone on a dessert Island.

Mavis: Yeah, me and that Sidney Pottery-a, or whatever he's called as well.

Sal: Well we're hardly a-bloody-lone there, with you and Sidney hanging around are we?

Mavis: Well we could be on the other side of the island. We wouldn't be in the way.

Sal: Why do you have to be on my island? Can't you be on your own island?.

Mavis: Well I'd get lonely there on me own with just Sidney. I do get lonely. I do, I like lots of company me.

Carol: Could me and Erik come too?

Sal: Bloody hell, I may as well stay here in the pub.

Mavis: Yeah, but it's a bit cold here too. It's cold like an igloo... can I still call them igloos?

ACT ONE SCENE FOUR – Evening Walk Home.

In the street, Ollie and his friends have left the Farmers Arms. Ollie is clearly drunk, Colin is tipsy.

Ollie: She's Lovely.

Colin: Who?

Ollie: That Janice, oh what I would do to get me hands on a bit of that.

Colin: You! (indignantly) She would look twice at you

Ollie: Why not?

Colin: Cause you're always pissed, that's why.

Ollie: She likes pissed men!

Colin: Why would she like pissed men?

Ollie: Because she's a f'kin barmaid, that's why, why would anyone become a f'kin barmaid unless they liked pissed men.

Colin: (Sarcastically) Duh! Maybe, because she needs a job..?

Ollie: Yeah, but she could get a job anywhere, she got a job at the farmers' because she likes pissed men!

Colin: Well let me see now, Janice is at the careers office back when she was sixteen and the careers officer say's "So, Janice what do you think you want to do with your life? " and Janice replies "well I quite like pissed men, so its barmaid for me" (Colin quotes Janice in a dippy girlie voice)

Ollie: Yeah!

Colin hangs his head and shakes it.

Colin: Well then why is it she used to work at the bookies then?

Ollie: 'Cause that's where pissed men go before they're pissed see! "shh shh" she's coming shush!.

Janice starts catching them up with a determined stride.

Ollie: Hiya love.

Janice slows to reply

Janice: Hiya Ollie, Colin.

Colin: Hiya, we were just talking about you.

Janice's eyes light up, she has a thing for Colin.

Janice: Nothing rude I hope

Ollie: No, No (embarrassingly)

Janice: Mores the pity.

Janice: Where's your Shelly tonight?

Ollie: Shelly Who?

Janice: Shelly your wife.

Ollie: Oh her, Christ I wouldn't be out tonight with her.

Janice: Why not?

Ollie: Its light nights. Jesus with a face like hers, I only take her out Halloween.

Janice: Oh don't be so mean.

Ollie: I'm not, it's not my fault she's ugly, it's in the genes see, she's turned into her mum, actually no she's turned into her dad, I don't mind the moustache that much, but the bald heads a right turn off.

Janice: Oh you love her really.

Ollie: Yeah, every Halloween, we go out collecting; she earns enough to pay for Christmas.

Colin interrupts.

Colin: So where are you off to?

Janice: Chippy, I'm starving, I ain't had now't all night.

Ollie: you "ain't had now't all night"....Well, I'll do my best love, but I'm in no fit state.

Colin: Ignore him, He's a bit pissed.

Janice: He's always a bit pissed

Ollie: I take great exception to that, I'm not a bit pissed, I'm fully pissed, I do nothing by halves.

Janice: I know, you do it all by pints.

Ollie: Seven, to be precise.

Janice: I know, I've been pulling them all night for you.

Ollie: (reaching down and fumbling with his fly) speaking of pulling something for me, would you...

Again Colin interrupts

Colin: Hey enough you idiot.

Janice: Don't worry Colin, Its nothing I can't handle.

Ollie: Yeah Colin, its nuffin' she can't handle. (he says with a wink)

Janice: Yes I've been told by the other girls "It Literally is...Nothing"

Ollie: What other girls?

Colin: Yeah exactly what other girls, the only other girl than Shelly that's seen his manhood lately was Pam and her five friends.

Ollie: I'll have you know my sexual prowess has always been met with the greatest of appreciation.

Colin: Yeah appreciated by the company who sells you your internet connection.

Janice: (to Ollie) Listen, why did you mention Dave Morley in the pub earlier?

Ollie: Cause I saw Bastard (beat, Ollie turns with a determined march off set) I need pies!

ACT ONE SCENE FIVE – Back At Chip Shop Counter.

Brian: Alright Col, Ol.

Colin/Ollie: (in synchronicity) El'reet Elvis

Marge: Alright Janice love, what you doing walking around with tweedle dumb and tweedle bloody dumber.

Ollie: That's a fine way to speak to your oldest customer.

Brian: (sings) Old sheppie has gone...(winks at Janice)

As the bell goes and Alice walks in, a seventy year old widower.

Ollie: Speaking of oldest customers, look at this walking in, fuck me there's pyramids younger than her.

Marge: Shut up you. Hiya Alice love.

Alice: Hiya, can a just have me single fish, n put a few scratchings in with it.

Ollie: Bloody hells bells, jump the queue why don't ya... Well now that I think about it, it's probably for the best she's got a bloody coffin going cold.

Marge: Strap yer face up you or you'll be out on yer ear.

Janice: (discreetly to Ollie) Tell me what you meant before!

Ollie: (Ignoring Janice) Sorry Margey, love, sweetheart, light of my life, beat of my heart, gravy of my Sunday roast, purveyor of clotted arteries and wise woman of the fryers.

He turns to Alice

Ollie: I'm only kidding, aye love I'm only kidding yer.

Alice: Your all right cock, I'll bloody outlive you anyways, I've seen me way through four husbands, two of them mine.

Ollie: (Laughing) See, she's a bit of a laugh, alright, you don't mind do you love am only having a giggle with you.

Marge: There you go love, single fish, plenty of scratchings. Two pounds fifty for you love.

Alice: Ooh, can I have a bottle of dandelion and burdock too please.

Marge: Certainly, We've only got the big bottles, One pound sixty five, is that alright.

Alice: It'll have to be, it's the only thing that settles my stomach after a fish supper.

Marge: Four pounds fifteen then please love.

Alice: Thank you.

Marge: Eighty five change, and here's your bag.

Brian: Have you lot decided yet?

Janice: Ollie..tell me what you meant.

Colin: (sings) There's a guy works down the chip shop swears he's Elvis.

Brian: I'll bloody Elvis you yer git!

Ollie: Taking care of business eh! Frying Tonight!!!

Janice: Look Tell me now!

Ollie: OK, OK for fuck sake. Brian, Marge...I saw Dave Morley earlier! Outside the farmers'.

Colin appears unaware; however Marge drops something and exits.

Brian: You're fucking joking (sternly)

Janice: When?

Ollie: Tonight ok, tonight, I saw him tonight, you know when I came in earlier Brian, the fucker was just outside. I didn't recognize him at first, it only struck me when he (points at Colin) mentioned Dozy Dave Gough.

Brian: Oh hey love... are you alright

Janice: (cries) No...and walks out stressed.

Colin glances for answers between Ollie and Brian before following.

Ollie: For fucks sake, this is why I didn't want to say owt.

Brian: You Twat!

Ollie: Shoot the messenger.

ACT ONE SCENE SIX – Back In The Street.
Colin: What's the matter?

Janice: (upset) Nothing, I have to get home now!

Colin: Let me walk with you then

Janice: Well walk fast.

Colin: So is he your boyfriend or something?

She stops

Janice: No!! (indignantly)

Colin: Then what's the matter? Who's Dave Morley?

Janice: It's nothing to do with you, I just don't want to say, alright.

Colin: I'm just trying to help.

Janice: How's this helping, your just being nosey. (angrily)

Colin: Fine (angrily)

Janice: Why the concern anyway? (softening)

Colin: I just, I'm just, well, I care okay!

Janice: Why? Why care, you don't hardly know me.

Colin: I do

Janice: Do you? How?, Every bloody guy who ever walks in the pub thinks they know me, thinks I'm their friend, thinks because I pay them ten seconds of attention I must fancy them, well I don't and I'm not, okay. They pay me, they pay me to smile, they pay me to listen to all your crap, and they pay me to put up with stupid drunk arse holes like your mate Bloody Ollie. But they don't know me. They don't know Janice, this Janice, Janice, who's doing her best to get on with her life. While she can, while SHE still has a life.

You want to know who Janice is, well I'll tell you who Janice is. Janice was the fiancée of some lad who eight years ago got killed by that bastard, Dave Morley.

Colin: Oh, Sorry Janice, I didn't know

Janice: Exactly, you didn't know and why should you, because YOU DON'T KNOW ME!

Colin: I wish I did.

Janice: What? Oh right, yeah, great just what I need right now!

Colin: You don't know me either, I'm not like Ollie, and I don't think you fancy me just because you smile when I buy a pint, I just know that I fancy you.

Sorry, your right that's not for now, I'm sorry it just came out, you must have other things on your mind.

Janice: Yes...No, it's alright carry on.

Colin: I can't its stupid, It wasn't meant to be like this, "I fancy you", I was hoping to... well under other circumstances, I just wanted to maybe... oh I don't know what I'm trying to say, I'm a bit pissed myself.

Janice: No, It's okay, I'm over reacting, He's out, and by the sound of things he's been out for a while, I don't know why I'm rushing, nothing's going to change.

Colin holds Janice by the elbows and pulls her closer. They look into each other's eyes when Ollie walks up.

Ollie: (sing) Two lovers entwine divine, divine. (changes song) Strangers in the night, exchanging fluids. What's going on here then, lovers tiff?

Colin: What do you think, she's upset that's all. (as Colin leads Ollie away from Janice)

Ollie: What about?

Colin: How can you bloody ask that, you must have known all along?

Ollie: She' got the painters in then, She on a red letter day?

Colin: You just have no fucking sensitivity do you, just do one will you.

Ollie: She asked the question. Why do I get the shite if she doesn't like the answer? Right, I'm going, I'll see you, see yer, and you love!

Janice: Who's he calling love?

Colin: Are you going to be alright? 'Tonight I mean, you're pretty shook up.

Janice: Yeah, I'll be fine, it's just thinking of him, that bastard, it brings it all back to me, you know.

Colin: I know, I couldn't imagine what you must be going through.

Janice: Most of the time, I can't imagine it myself; it's like it's someone else's thoughts. Gordon was his name. I was with him for four years, the last two engaged.

Colin: Oh!

Janice: He was Brian and Marge's son.

Colin: Hmm, yeah I heard their son got killed, just didn't know the details I suppose, God such a shame.

Janice: Well, yes, for them maybe.

Colin: What about you?

Janice: Yes, for me to, but more for them, he was their son.

Colin: Aye, but for Christ's sake you were going to marry him, you must have been devastated.

Janice: I suppose, but it nearly killed Marge, literally, she took it bad.

Colin: Well I'm sorry for not knowing.

Janice: See; look at you, all humble it has a way of changing things doesn't it, something like that. Something significant eight years ago. It changes who I am, who Marge is, and look you enter this world of mine just a moment ago and already you're changed, humbled, cautious.

Colin: I don't know what to say.

Janice: There is nothing you can say, sorry…why it wasn't your fault, why do we say sorry to someone when we learn of a death.

Colin: Empathy I suppose.

Janice: Anyway I thought you were walking me home; we'll not get far stood here talking.

ACT ONE SCENE SEVEN – Chip Shop Counter.

Marge: I'm alright now you soft get.

Brian: You sure.

Marge: (wipes her nose) yeah, whoa (sigh) I so miss him you know.

Brian: I know love

Marge: we'll be alright won't we?

Brian: Yeah, we'll be alright.

Marge: he was still a baby.

Brian: he was a man.

Marge: He was my baby.

Brian: Mine too, but you know love, things happen.

Marge: How can you say that?

Brian: He'd grown up sweetheart.

Marge: No, he hadn't, not for me, all I remember is whipping his nose, whipping his arse, fastening his laces, cutting his hair and seeing him in that bloody hospital. Why do all my memories end in that one hey? Why?

Brian: I know love, I know.

Marge: how does it happen, Brian?

Brian: (comforts Marge) I know.

Marge: And then the bastard has the nerve to go to the farmers, THE FARMERS ! it's one hundred yards away from us, and he has the bollocks to stagger into our local like butter wouldn't fucking melt, knowing! Knowing! That we're here and knowing what he'd done to us, to our Gordon.

Brian: I know love, maybe he wasn't thinking.

Marge: "Wasn't thinking!" how can he not be thinking, its all I ever think of, how can he not be thinking of it. He knew, He knew it, but he didn't care.

Brian: Look I'll speak to the police tomorrow, see if I can get an injunction out or 'summat'.

Marge: What kind of a man, could do that, come here and rub our noses in it. (sigh) ooh, Gordon!

Brian: (wipes her tear, looks sternly at her putting on his brave face but lovingly) Come on love, let's focus, nothing's changed, we cope, this is what we do.

Marge: Yeah (sniff) we'll be alright.

Brian: (sings to Marge) crying (smiles) crying, crying, I'll be crying o'o'over yooooou!

Marge: You'll be crying in the spare room tonight if you don't get cracking. She smiles back

Brian: You just get on with emptying those scoops, and then fill the salt and vinegars up.

Another customer walks in

Brian: Only puddings and battered sausages left now mate.

Marge: Speak for yourself.

Craig: No chips?

Brian: Nope, we've cleaned down mate.

Craig: Go on then, I'll have a pudding.

Marge: Ninety five pence then tar love.

Brian: (sings) working nine teee' five...

Marge: Will you quit it with the stupid songs.

Brian: I've always been like this, ever since we met, you said you loved my singing.

Marge: That was before, before you sang twenty four hours a day, seven days a week, I can't get a bloody word out of you unless you sing it.

Brian: (Sings) It's only words, and words are not enough...

Marge: enough... enough! Words are bloody enough, shush will you!

Marge turns back to Craig

Marge: Ninety Five ta!

Craig: Marge? Marge Reynolds?

Marge: Yeah! Well Langley now, since I married Brian 'Elvis' Langley here, sorry do I know you?

Craig: You should, we went out ooh, for all of two weeks, when was that, It'd be oh nineteen seventy eight, you were about sixteen.

Brian: (sings) She was sixteen, she was beautiful, now she's mine all mine.

Marge: I don't remember you at all?

Craig: Well you wouldn't really, I was very different then, Craig's the name, Craig Hennessey.

Marge: Craig Hennessey, Craig bloody Hennessey, Yeah, I do remember you.

Brian: I remember you-oo, you're the one.

Marge: Brian for God's sake. Last I heard of you you'd joined the army or something.

Craig: Well not really, TA, but I was a prison warden in real life. Then I moved to Sheffield.

Marge: Well you look like you're doing well for yourself, you've kept yourself trim.

Brian: Bloody hell calm down Marge love. Don't worry it's the menopause mate!

Marge: You know what, it's like having one of those bloody talking birds on me shoulder, I feel like long john bleeding silver, will you pack in chirping in, I'm trying to have a conversation here !

Brian: Sorry I spoke!

Marge: Well it's nice seeing you love, hope things are all okay for you.

Craig: Oh, I'm sure you'll be seeing me again, I've moved back here now.

Craig leaves

Brian: That's cheered you up, Look at you, you've gone all flush.

Marge: Don't be stupid.

Brian: You have your all red and embarrassed

Marge: I'm not, I've just been crying you soft get anyway what've I got to be embarrassed about.

Brian: Him, "Craig", what's that all about then.

Marge: Get away with you! Two bloody weeks, thirty bleeding years ago. I should be so lucky, look at him, look at me; I'm twice the size I was back then.

Brian: See, given half the chance you'd be in there like a shot.

Marge: No I'm just saying, even if I was single, what do you think he'd see in me now days.

Brian: Probably the same girl he saw thirty years ago.

Marge: Yeah Right!

Brian: Why not, I do.

Marge: Oh come here you sweetheart.

Brian: Soft git!

Marge: My soft git.

Brian: (sings) Young girl....get outta my mind...my love for you is way outta line. (Brian slaps Marge on the bottom) better run girl, your much too young girl..

She smiles and runs off set, Brian chases, laughing. The door bell rings and Mavis, Sal & Carol Walk in.

Brian: Evening girls, out on the razzle again I see.

Mavis: Ooh you don't know the half of it, do you hear, you don't know the half of it.

Brian: I bet I can guess with you lot, no mans safe when you lot are together.

Sal: Not if he's a rich and famous black man

Mavis, Sal, Carol: (Giggle)

Brian: Bloody hell Sal, calm down, what is it with you women tonight, your all on bloody heat. It's bad enough with the wild woman of Borneo here, lusting after an old flame, then you three walk in, no wonder my bloody windows are all steamed up.

Marge: I WAS NOT lusting, I didn't even remember him.

Carol: Oooh goss! , come on Marge fill me in, I want all the details, who, when where, and most importantly how big!

Marge: Ooh, you lot, I wouldn't have a clue, I was sweet and innocent back then.

Brian: You act like your sweet an innocent now, well it feels like it. You know it's strange, you women, you hold out until we promise to marry you, then we get twelve months of three times a day, then once you get a bloody ring on your fingers, it's like a bloody giro, you get it once a fortnight and you have to bend over backwards otherwise your claim gets dismissed.

Marge: Well in your case love it's less of a giro, more of a disability benefit.

Sal: Well I must be on knob seekers allowance then (laughs).

Brian: Well you'll have to make do with a battered jumbo sausage, it's all that's left.

Sal: Story of my life, anyway Marge, when are you going to get out with us.

Marge: What and leave him on his own..in here..with sharp objects.

Carol: Are you two having anything, or is it just me.

Sal: Oh go on then, I'll have some chips.

Mavis: we could just get a big bag between us.

Sal: no I don't want to start mine till I get home, I'll have 'em on a butty.

Mavis: I think they sell bread here, you do don't you Marge, sell bread here?

Sal: I'm not going to try to assemble a butty while I'm walking home, it's hard enough trying to walk as it is in these bloody shoes, besides, this is a new top, you know me I'll end up with butter all down me front.

Marge: There's, no chips anyways, we've cleaned down now.

Sal: Bloody hell, I was just in the mood for some chips then too, what have you?

Marge: Steak and Kidney Puddings, three battered sausages or I can warm you a pie up in the micro.

Mavis: Meat and p'tater please.

Sal: Aye Same here.

Carol: Well give us a couple of them battered sausages, I'll take one home for Erik.

Marge: Separate?

Carol: No

Marge: I'll put the three in and charge for two, it'll only go to waste. Put a couple of meat and taters in please Brian. One eighty please Carol. Yours are a pound each. Here guess what he's gone and done, he's only bloody ordered a kebab machine.

Carol: ooh them spicy things, oh I can't eat anything spicy me.

Sal: Oh I can, I like a nice chilli.

Mavis: I know, but not as much as the Farmers.

Carol: Why do they like them a lot?

Mavis: Who?

Carol: The farmers.

Mavis: No, I said "it's not as cold in here as it is the farmers". You're not listening again, I said she never listens.

Brian: I can't follow you lots conversations. I swear you talk in some sort of old woman code; you switch from one subject to the next like your changing channel on the bloody TV.

Sal: That's because us women can multitask, you men! You can only do one thing at a time, anymore and you get all confused.

Brian: Multi-tasking my arse, you can do any two things simultaneously; as long as one of them is giving it that (he does a hand puppet talking motion). Besides I can do more than two things at once.

Marge: Yeah, flick through the channels and scratch your arse, while your legs are shaking like a dog on heat. What is it with men? Why do they do that? Sit there either scratching their nuts or shaking their legs while the telly is on, they can't sit still their always doing something to annoy you.

Brian: Look who's talking, your bloody breathing annoys me, but despite my objections you do keep doing it.

Sal: Well it doesn't look like you're going to get any tonight Marge.

Marge: Wouldn't be getting any anyways, he's semi retired.

Sal: Eh?

Marge: Well he only ever had a semi, now even that's retired.

Brian: Well if he only ever had a semi, you'll have to ask yourself "why is it that? –that's all you could inspire?"

Marge: Aye well you didn't seem to complain at the time.

Brian: I never needed to, you do enough complaining for the both of us.

Sal,Carol & Mavis: ooooohhh!!! (meow style)

Marge: Well you give me plenty to complain about.

Carol: Oh don't start rowing you two, you were all lovey dovey when we came in.

Brian: Oh don't threat yourself, were always like this, it's what keeps us on our toes.

Marge: Yeah.

Mavis: It's her (pointing at Sal) she could start a fight in a monastery this one.

Sal: It weren't me, Christ you'd have me shot for a lion one day.

Mavis: I know I would, I'd be doing the shooting too if you don't get a move on.

Sal: See you later kidders

Group: See ya!

ACT ONE SCENE EIGHT – Dave Morley's Monologue.

I have killed, I am a killer. Dave's the name, Dave Morley. I wasn't always a killer; fifteen years ago I was a student. I was studying law ironically enough. Before that, a kid at school, I wasn't a bully or anything like that, I've not had a difficult upbringing either, my parents were very-very average, well apart from the fact that I had two, I suppose that's pretty weird today.

I know what they all thought of me, Bastard. That's what you all thought, you see us killers are stereotyped, it's the movies that do it, and the telly, but you know what sometimes we just end up in situations, in places we never intended. Sometimes we come out as hero's, sometimes as villains, it just depends on the timing that's all or the flip of a coin.

Me, I always saw me-self as an hero, I always imagined that when the shit hit the fan I would be there, like a shining beacon, running in to the burning house, picking up the kid then going back for the mum. Firemen patting me on the back, local paper writing a story about me, Dave Morley, local hero. I can swim too, I'd be there wading in helping the fukin' idiot who fell in probably while pissing about with his mates.

Or when the gang of skins were beating up some paki lad, just because he's not white, see I'm against all that shit, I'd be there proving that were not all twats, some Brits do care about others, not in your namby pamby liberal loony way.

They'd be running around like wannabe fucking nazi's all shaved heads and braces, somehow reinforcing their self-inflated supremacy by outnumbering some poor paki kid and I'd run across the road and deck one of them, one punch, down, and the rest would run off, that's how I saw it like, in me little head like.

But now I'm just killer, bastard or killer bastard, (shakes head) killer.

It has its plus points I suppose, I get a lot of respect I never got before, you see killer goes before Dave in some sort of mixed up definition of who I am.

I have a mum, honest I do, I have a mum and she gave birth to me, I wasn't created by society or a result of some evil experiment.

Killers, and trust me I know a few now, well sometimes they just happen through no fault of their own.

I once cried that my dad died, I cried that my dog died, I ran crying to my mum when a bee stung me back when I was seven or eight.

When do you think was the last time I cried?

See you're starting to see ME now aren't you? You're having second thoughts. See that's real second thoughts, second thoughts really are thinking over the same subject twice, not just having doubts, too many people say they're having second thoughts when in fact they were unsure about something from the start, you now are having real second thoughts, your opinion may have changed a little.

The killer is fading and the person is emerging, you realize that maybe I'm more than just a stereotypical movie style bad guy...go on, guess, when was the last time I cried?

Wait, stop that, your picturing me as a child.

Stop it.

Picture me now, when was the last time I cried in this bulk of a frame...that's better you're looking at me and can see my tears.

Yes its now. I'm crying now.

Maybe there's no visible tears from where you sit or maybe just a smidgeon, but I am crying now, and I cry every fucking night. I cry so much I think I've actually lost weight in tears.

See me, I'm a fucking hero.

I have killed, I took a life, but I'm not a bastard, I'm an unlucky hero.

That fucker who I killed, I cry for, but more so I cry for myself too. I cry more for me who's stuck in this fucking miserable life while he has escaped.

He was a bastard he was. Course you won't hear that in the paper, they always take the "victims" side, they say how he was a friendly, fun loving family man, much missed son and I become the villain. See the headline "Hero kills boy 19 in one punch" doesn't ring right does it? Everything needs to be black and white in a newspaper. But it is true he didn't deserve to die. I was a hero, but more than he didn't deserve to die, I didn't deserve to kill him.

I hit him and I was being a hero. That was my job, Hero. I helped remove from the bar four wankers that night. But one of them, just one of them, the last one obviously, took his lighter to the hair of this girl. She had hair some hair lacquer on it or something, it went up like a fucking petrol bomb. Course we put it out quick, she didn't even get burned, just a bit singed.

She was alright.

I took him outside he was like "paki bitch, paki that, get the fuck out of our country" she wasn't even Pakistani though turns out she was from somewhere else, can't remember now, further east, thick bastard that he was, so yeah I fucking decked him alright. Adrenaline kicked in, see as soon as you break that invisible barrier ejecting the riff raff, it takes a while to come back up, you still feel like the situation is on...you know what I mean.

Neither was the he even a member of any right wing organization it turns out, he was just showing off. That and she happened to be sat with a lad who jumped for joy as Man U came back to score two goals in the final to win the treble, and this knob head was a Chelsea supporter...Now don't get me wrong I'm anyone but Man U too but you know, its just a game.

You see he thought it was alright to say such fucking evil things, his mates jeered him on, he takes it a bit further, he' starts believing some of the shite he comes out with because it gets affirmation. The further he took it the more it became right, is like a spiral upwards instead of downwards.

Anyway I lost my rag, I'd had these principles all my life, it was time to stand up and be the hero.

One punch, smack...... dead, it's not like he even hit his head on the pavement or on the grate like they do in crappy murder programs. No blood, couldn't even see a fucking bruise.

You see, it's not just that some people don't know their own strength, truth is, we don't know other people weaknesses, sometimes people we don't realize how frail they are, people are frail.

A tiny smack causes a bruise, which causes a clot, which causes a stroke, which causes a death.

Think about that next time you wanna' smack someone, even if they are being a cunt.

Sorry for my language missus, I can't help it now days it's who I am, and sorry, you know for using the P' word, I don't mean it like them fucking retards do, I don't mean it to put anyone down, to me it's just a name, I could say Asian, Indian or Pakistani, but then it wouldn't be natural from my lips, no more than me trying to speak like fucking Shakespeare.

See with me it's not what you say, but in what context it is said.

I meant no disrespect.

(Fade.)

ACT TWO

The Chip Shop is at first empty. Brian enters he is whistling Love Me Tender and carrying a metal bucket and mop. But he is less cheerful than previously. The whistling seems contrived as if trying to lift his spirits. He goes in front of the counter places the bucket on the floor and the mop he props up against the counter. Marge enters she looks tired. She hardly acknowledges Brian. Brian continues whistling. He grabs hold of the mop but seems reluctant to start the sweeping of the floor.

MARGE: Can we have one day without bleedin' Elvis.

BRIAN: (stops whistling) You okay Love. I know you had trouble sleeping.

MARGE: And why do you think that. Noticed nothing troubling you.

BRIAN: It's not this Dave Morley business is it.

MARGE: What do you think?

BRIAN: We've only Ollie's word for any of this and since when did you take any notice of an old soak like Ollie

MARGE: I know Dave Morley is out there.

BRIAN: How can you know that?

MARGE: I just do. Isn't it stirring you up an all? I mean doesn't it bring it all back

BRIAN: I like to keep myself busy. What good does thinking do me? I left it all behind.

MARGE: (angry) How can you leave it all behind. The man that murdered our son is wondering about without a care in the world and you want to play with a mop and whistle Elvis songs.

BRIAN: What would you have me do?

MARGE: For a start act as if you had a son once.

BRIAN: Now you know that's out of order.

MARGE: Is it? Even at the funeral you didn't seem to care. I let it go cos I thought you were just trying to be strong. Christ I knew I couldn't be. But no looking back I see now you just didn't give a damn.

BRIAN: (controlled anger) You know that isn't true.

MARGE: Do I

BRIAN: It's complicated I cried for him. More than you know.. (Brian pauses then seems to forget himself) I grieved for him even before he died.

MARGE: What the hell is that suppose to mean.

BRIAN: Look I can't tell you. You wouldn't want to know even if you did want to listen, which you don't. Keep your perfect little memories. He stopped being your angelic little boy a long time before he died.

MARGE: How can you stand there and speak like that about your own flesh and blood.

BRIAN: Forget I said owt you're usually good at that. Why don't you just go and sit in that shrine of a room you've kept up there for the last 8 years?

MARGE: Sod this I'm going out.

BRIAN: You what.

MARGE: I'm not standing here listening to your bile a moment longer.

Marge strides out from behind counter and exits.

ACT TWO SCENE TWO – BREAKFAST AT JANICE'S

Janice's dad is sat in an armchair, reading a paper; mum is off in the kitchen unseen

Mum: (from back) You getting up love

Janice: (from back) Yes, I'll be down in a minute.

Dad: What is this bloody world coming to?

Janice sits down on the chair, dad looks up at her.

Dad: You were late in.

Janice: Oh, I just got talking.

Dad: Tell yer mum put the kettle on.

Janice: You do it.

Dad: I just did.

Janice: What did she say then?

Dad: Same as you.

Janice: What?

Dad: she said "you do it."

Janice: Well so you should.

Dad: Oh go-on she'll do it for you.

Janice: probably, but don't you think its time you got of your arse and made mum a cup of tea once in a while.

Mum: (walking in the room) you all right love.

Janice: yeah, tired a bit.

Mum: You see anyone.

Janice: Colin Frogall.

Dad: Any relation to Barry Frogall.

Janice: Yeah, that's his dad.

Dad: Bloody hell Barry Frogall, what a nutter he was.

Mum: Is that him in the wheelchair.

Dad: Yeah, fucking funny that was

Mum: oh don't be cruel you, there but for the grace of god.

Dad: Well it is funny, bloody Barry Frogall will be the first to tell you.

Janice: Why what happened.

Dad: Well back in his day, Barry was a right fucking raver. Course I'm going back to the early eighties now.

Janice: yeah...

Dad: Well Barry goes to this rock concert, can't remember who, Alice cooper or that Ozzy fellah. Well he'd been going to rock concerts since the sixties, like I said he was a right raver, and back then, if you could you'd run up on stage, hug the guitarist or singer, or whatever, then go crowd surfing.

Janice: Crowd surfing?

Dad: Yeah, you know, you jump of the stage into the crowd, who lift you and push you around the front of the stage.

Janice: Oh yeah, yeah I know what you mean.

Dad: Well, Barry gets up on the stage, shows his arse to the crowd or whatever then turns around in triumph, he then spots this crowd of head bangers near the front of the stage, waving and beckoning him, so he thinks they're calling him over for a crowd surf.

Janice: Weren't they?

Dad: I don't know, all I know is that nowadays they're all politically correct at concerts and so they ship all the people in wheelchairs in front of the stage, Barry dives in without realizing, sends fucking wheelchairs all over the show. They had to get an ambulance to him, he ended up in one himself, broke his back. Ironic isn't it.

Mum: Ooh that's awful.

Dad: It was him who told me, he thought it was funny too.

Janice: He's probably just putting a brave face on it.

Dad: Oh, he's hard as fucking nails him.

Mum: No it's you, you never have any consideration for others, what was it the other day, when we were in B&Q?

Dad: My point exactly, Bloody B&Q having disabled spaces right outside the door.

Janice: So?

Dad: So if they can bloody "do it themselves" why do they need special bloody parking spaces? Don't get me wrong, I'm not having a go at them, its B&Q, I mean, they'll give them special spaces right in front of the shop, but then they don't have any consideration once you're in there.

Ikea's the worst, they put disabled spaces right in front of the doors, for what... to make the distance disabled people struggle into the shop shorter... then once you're in there, they still have to walk the same ten miles around the shop as the rest of us, it's just a ploy to make themselves look caring.

Janice: God he's off on one now.

Dad: I'm just saying that's all.

Mum: Do you want a cuppa tea love

Janice: Go on then ta!

Dad: 'Bout bloody time too, I'm parched here.

Mum: No you're bloody perched there, it's about time you made one.

Dad: Oh for Christ's sake, I don't know why I bother having a chair I never get five minutes, just sat watching telly.

Dad gets up to make teas, Janice and mum smile knowingly at each other.

Mum: So what's he like this Colin Frogall.

Janice: Oh you must know him; he used to knock around with Gary Kent when he was smaller.

Mum: Oh, the lad always wore denims, and socks on the outside of his jeans.

Janice: They were leg warmers, it was the fashion.

Mum: I thought he was a girl at first.

Janice: Oh mum we all dressed like that then.

Mum: That's what I mean, you couldn't tell who was boys or girls back then.

Dad comes back through.

Dad: Kettles on.

He sits.

Dad: What was I on about?

Mum: When?

Dad: Just now

Mum: Tea?

Dad: No before that

Mum: People in wheelchairs.

Dad: That was it, yeah, Barry Frogall.

Janice rolls her eyes

Dad: Oh I can tell you another story about that one.

Janice: Go on then!

Dad: Well there's me and him in a nightclub, this is before I met your mam and we're sat there in suits, you had to wear suits back then to get into a nightclub, tie and everything.

Anyway, were sat there in our suits and its early, cause there's not many people in. that and it was a Thursday and I'd just got me dole so I had a couple of quid, whereas he had none.

After about an hour, the place isn't picking up and there's only one or two people in, but there is these two girls. So since were the only two single fellas in the place and these are the only two girls, we go across and sit at their table.

Do you still get tables in nightclubs now? (doesn't wait for an answer).

Well we sit there and after a bit of small talk I buy a round, and we keep talking.

Course girls never bought rounds then and when this one finished it would have been Barry's turn to get them in.

But I knew he had no money, and so thinking if he embarrasses me by saying he's got no money, we'll have blown it with these two bits of skirt.

So I take a fiver out of me' pocket, and subtly place it in his jacket pocket which was hung over his chair.

I nudge him and say "Are you going to get them in then Barry?"

And then he goes "I can't I don't have any money"

Playing it down and making a joke of it I say, "You do, you've got that bloody fiver in your jacket pocket" and give him a knowing nod.

Then he reaches in the pocket, pulls out this fiver, looks at me, and do you know what the little bastard said…." Bloody hell I didn't know I had that, I'll keep that for Saturday night!"

What a bloody idiot!...me an all!

Mum: serves you bloody right, skirt chasing.

Janice: Where's this tea then dad? I've got to be off.

Dad: alright, alright

Dad gets up and goes in the back again.

Mum: You got bus fair?

Janice: No it's alright I've got a lift.

Mum: A lift? Who from?

Janice: Just someone.

Mum: Just someone eh?

Janice smiles

Mum: That wouldn't be anyone we've just been talking about would it?

Janice: It might. (Janice solemns her expression pauses) Dave Morley's out apparently.

Mum: Never!

Janice: Seems so.

Mum: how do you feel?

Janice: I'm alright. Just brings it all back that's all.

Mum: Well he did you a bloody favour if you ask me.

Janice: Oh mum how can you say that?

Mum: You know.

Janice: I know what?

Mum: You think I'm bloody blind don't you.

Janice: It wasn't like that.

Mum: Look everyone round here has this glossy memory of poor bloody Gordon but me.

Janice: Mum! urgh !

Mum: It's no good getting annoyed at me. He changed you, it's took till this long to get my Janice back.

Janice: He didn't change me, I loved him.

Mum: Maybe you did, but did he love you? Because if he did he had a funny bloody way of showing it.

Janice: I don't wanna talk about it.

Mum: It's about time you did, look, you've just told me your meeting this lad, it's the first one you have shown any interest in eight bloody years, you can't tell me that was just grief.

Janice: Nothing happened okay.

Mum: Right ! Fine! But don't blame me for trying to care about you.

ACT TWO SCENE THREE-Ollie Brian in street.

Ollie: Hey Brian, Sorry about that last night and all.

Brian: Nah, yer alright lad, not your fault, just a sensitive issue that's all.

Ollie: Well tell Marge sorry for me will you.

Brian: I will, but really you were right, we shot the messenger, it was just a bit of a shock really, then Marge getting all upset like that, caught me on the back foot, so it's me who should say sorry to you mate.

Ollie: Don't worry about it mate, I was a bit pissed, went in one ear and out the other.

Brian: Was Janice okay?

Ollie: I reckon so, Col took her home.

Brian: 'Tut'. Great.

Ollie: What?

Brian: That's all Marge needs.

Ollie: What?

Brian: Janice, moving on like!.

Ollie: Come on Brian, she can't stay celibate, she's a young lass.

Brian: I know, it's not me, its Marge isn't it, I don't know where we are lately, one minute were all over each other, next minute well I'm out here walking it off ain't I, anyway she sees Janice as a link don't she, if Janice changes, moves on, well that's just another kick in the teeth ain't it.

Ollie: Bloody hell.

Brian: I know.

Ollie: Women!

Brian: Aye!

Ollie: They've always got sommat to sulk about.

Brian: Bloody Librans!

Ollie: Ay?

Brian: Librans, they have this star sign looks like a pair of scales, to them they think it means their all well adjusted, balanced, neutral.

Ollie: Oh right.

Brian: Yeah, but it doesn't mean that at all:

Ollie: No?

Brian: No, it means they bloody swing from one side to the other...there's never any bloody balance.

Ollie: Aye!

Brian: Aye!

(beat)

Ollie: So what star sign are you then Brian?

Brian: Me, Cancer!

Ollie: Oh right, crabby then.

Brian: Nah mate, rotting from the inside out.

Ollie: Must be hard though mate.

Brian: What living with me.

Ollie: No, Gordon and all.

Brian: Apple of her eye weren't he.

Ollie: I don't know how you coped.

Brian: Well, like I say Marge took it bad.

Ollie: What about you?

Brian: Yeah, it was hard, but for different reasons.

Ollie: I don't know what you mean.

Brian: You know what he was like.

Ollie: I know, but he weren't a bad lad really.

Brian: He was my son, and I loved him so I can say nothing bad about him. And given the chance I'd do anything to have him back, but only so maybe I could fix whatever the hell it was that got into him.

Ollie: Brian, Jesus man.

Brian: I know, I can't help it though, don't you say a word to Marge mind you.

Ollie: Of course, Jesus Brian what do you think I am, I'm your mate aren't I.

Brian: I know.

Ollie: Well surely Marge knew he weren't a saint.

Brian: She saw it, but somehow, she didn't see it, do you know what I mean?

ACT TWO SCENE FOUR — WALKING IN THE STREET.

Sal: Always moaning she's bloody cold, I don't know why we put up with her. And if she says something once she says it a bloody dozen times.

Carol: Well she old isn't she.

Sal: Is she hell, she's only a couple of years over me.

Carol eyes up Sal and decides not to comment

And she gets you just like her, she never hears what you say first time, so you end up repeating yourself just as much as her.

Carol: Well she's a bit deaf ain't she?

Sal: Is she heckers like, she only hears what she wants to hear, I tell you, doesn't matter how quiet you offer her a stout, she hears that clear as daylight

Carol: clear as a bell.

Sal: Well you know what I mean. And on top of that..oooh she is a gossip, I mean I'm not one to talk. But I tell you if you're not there, I bet your ears are burning.

Carol: Why what she said about me.

Sal: Well I don't mean you in particular, I mean if anyone's not there, I mean if it was just me and her now, like this, then she'd be on about you.

Carol: Yeah, So what she said.

Sal: Well I'm not one for spreading gossip, so I don't like to say, I just take it with a pinch of salt. But I say what I think I do.

Carol: I know you do.

Sal: If I have something to say, I'll say it to your face.

Carol: Oh I know (rolling her eyes).

Sal: Give us another one of those glassier mints (a beat) I'm sure they were bigger when I was little

Carol: Yeah, That's that global warming done that. Its melting the glaciers (laughs)

Sal: (missing the joke entirely) is it? Ooh, you'd think they'd make them cheaper then wouldn't you.

Mavis: Hiya girls, ooh its bloody cold today isn't it. I've got two cardies on and I'm still cold you know.

Sal: Hiya Mavis, Carol was just talking about you. I say speak of the devil.

Mavis: I thought my ears were burning.

Carol: Well at least your ears would be warm hey Mavis:

Mavis: Oh no bloody freezing, I've got two cardies on and I'm still cold.

Sal: Ay, what about that then, Dave Morley.

Carol: Oh I know, shocking ain't it?

Mavis: Such a shame

Sal: Life should mean life; look at him only did seven years for murder!

Carol: Manslaughter.

Sal: I don't know what the difference is to be honest.

Carol: Murder is when you intend to kill someone, and manslaughter is when you don't.

Mavis: BLOODY HELLS BELLS!

Carol: What?

Mavis: Well that's just the bloody way this government works isn't it!

Carol: No, It's always been like that.

Mavis: So what your saying is I could get more bloody time in prison than someone who's killed someone?

Sal: What the hell are you on about?

Mavis: Well you just said, Murder is when you intend to kill someone, and that manslaughter is when you don't.

Carol: Yes?

Mavis: Well bloody hell, I intended to kill my Ralph for most of our bloody marriage.

Sal: Oh you soft get!

Carol: If you intend to kill them and actually do!

Mavis: Oh, ay I thought that was a bit unfair. Such a shame though.

Sal: I know

Mavis: Such a young lad.

Sal: Yes I know

Mavis: You don't feel safe to walk the streets these days with all these 'Huggies'.

Sal: Hoodies

Mavis: That's what I said. You just don't feel safe to walk the streets at night anymore.

Carol: I didn't know you'd be doing that at your age (winking at Sal).

Mavis: Well you could when we were young its just not the same anymore, my back door was always open.

Sal and Carol erupt into laughter

Sal: No, she meant like you were walking the street, you know, a street walker.

Mavis: That's what I said; we could when we were young.

Sal: No, oh never mind.

Mavis: I know what she bloody meant, she meant walking the streets like a prostitute! Well I wasn't always a bloody shrivelled prune you know!

Sal and Carol look at each other incredulously.

ACT TWO SCENE FIVE– Marge's Shrine.

Marge is knelt near a small table with a photograph and a candle on it, she has a tear in her eye. Brian enters.

Brian: Bloody hell love. We were okay, nothing's changed, I thought you were through this.

Marge: I am, I am.

Brian: What the bloody hell did he have to come back for and start this all off again?

Marge: It's my baby.

Brian: Marge, love, come on.

Marge: I want my baby.

Brian: I know love, I know, He's probably looking at you now saying "get up you daft get, I'm alright"

Marge: I know, it's me though.

Brian: He's not suffering love.

Marge: I am, I'm suffering, I want my baby back.

Brian: He was a grown man

Marge: Not to me, you don't understand.

Brian: Course I do.

Marge: It's not the same

Brian: Course it the bloody same, he was my son too.

Marge: But you never loved him like I did.

Brian: How can you say that!

Marge: You were always having a go at him, nothing he ever did was right.

Brian: Nothing he ever did WAS RIGHT!

Marge: See.

Brian: Yes I did SEE, YOU, It was YOU that didn't see.

Marge: What didn't I see?

Brian: Him, Oh you put him up there on your little bloody pedestal, look at you, kneeling in front of it like that, but you knew he was a bad'un.

Marge: Maybe if you could have shown a bit of love once in a while.

Brian: I did show love, Christ woman I showed nothing but love, but he shit all over me, and he shit all over you too, I stuck up for you!

Marge: I never asked you to.

Brian: What am I supposed to do!

Marge: He was your son!

Brian: And I had to choose, between him and you.

Marge: I would always choose my bloody kids.

Brian: So would I, but not when they're in the wrong and not when they are wronging you.

Marge: There is no right or wrong!

Brian: There is when he punches you in the stomach.

Marge: That was an accident.

Brian: Aye, I suppose it was an accident when Janice had that bloody cast on her arm for two months.

Marge: She fell getting out of the bath

Brian: Yes that's what she told you, she fell a lot didn't she

Marge: He didn't do all that!

Brian: See, "All that". Course he bloody did, He was always hurting someone, one way or a-bloody-nother, always hurting someone.

Marge: You hated him

Brian: I never did, but that little bugger had me in turmoil.

Marge: He didn't deserve to bloody die though did he?

Brian: No, no he didn't. But YOU need to move on.

Marge: I can't.

Brian: You can.

Marge: I don't want to…. Oh why did that bastard come back?

Brian: Maybe so we could get this out in the bloody open.

Marge: What?

Brian: This!

Marge: This what?

Brian: This, what you're doing, we need to get up, straighten ourselves out, and carry on. Dave Morley is a Bastard, for coming here and raking this all up again.. but god damn it, he's done his time and you know what?

Marge: What?

Brian: I believe him, I believed him all along! , there it's said now!

Marge: You two faced bastard!

Brian: Yes, yes I'm two faced; I have had one face for you these past bloody ten years nearly. Pretending Gordon was an innocent victim, caught up in a bloody fight he had nothing to do with, but I knew the truth and, if truth be known, I think you bloody did too, He bloody started trouble wherever he went.

Marge: Get out.

Brian: You need to face up to it girl.

Marge: Get out!

Brian: I'll get out, but as god is my witness this needed to be said.

Marge: Yeah, go, walk away again! That's what your good at.

Brian: yeah and one of these days it will be "one time too many".

> Smoke fills the stage, orange lights flickering in the background, people are stood around backs to the audience. Colin can be seen at the back, his arm around Janice.
>
> Crackles and fire sounds. Ollie wanders up.

Ollie: Bloody hell what's going on here then?

Colin: Bloody fire isn't it.

Ollie: I can see it a bloody fire, I mean you two arm in arm.

Janice: What do you bloody think it is?

Ollie: So anyone inside?

Colin: Dunno?

Ollie: Well has anyone checked?

Janice: Who's gonna bloody go in there and look, you?

Ollie: Yeah!

Colin: Oh Aye!

Ollie: Seriously, there could be kids in there or anything.

Janice: Don't think so this old house, doesn't look like anyone's lived there in years.

Ollie: Well I'm not taking that chance.

Colin: Yeah yeah, Ollie Dunbar, local hero, more likely run in to save a bottle of whiskey.

Ollie runs into the smoke.

Colin: Jesus Ollie, I thought you were joking.

Janice: I don't believe it, He'll be bloody killed, the flames are pouring out the windows.

Colin: Ollie, come back you idiot.

Sirens sound as a fire engine arrives, blue flashing lights through the smoke.

Fireman1: Stand back, Stand back!

Fireman2: Is there anyone in there?

Colin: Yeah, my mate, the idiot's just ran in to see if there is anyone in there.

Fireman2: Well there bloody is now then isn't there.

An explosion can be heard, breaking glass, the roars of flame get louder

Fireman2: What's his name?

Colin: Ollie, Oliver Dunbar.

Fireman2 heads over to fireman1

Fireman2: Right were gonna need the breathing apparatus, seems some idiot has run in.

Just then the crowd parts as Ollie covered in out brings out Alice covered in a blanket coughing and spluttering.

Colin: Ollie!

Fireman2: Stand back, stand back!

Janice: Bloody hells bells Ollie!

Fireman1: Ok mate, we'll take her from here.

Alice: You will bloody hell!

Colin: Ollie I don't bloody believe it.

Alice: I tell you what, I thought that was it till this fella came along.

One of the crowds produces a wheelchair for Alice to sit on, the firemen disappear into the smoke with their hoses. Ollie puts his arm around Alice's back

Ollie: Now then love, you'll be alright now.

Alice looks up at him.

Alice: I survived the bloody blitz, two divorces and bloody heart bypass, but I swear that time I thought that was it for me, I couldn't even see my own stairs in a house I've lived in for forty two years. Son, you are a bleeding angel sent from God.

Janice: Yeah, Ollie, you're a hero, did you know that, a real hero.

Alice: Oh, look at me poor house. What will I do?

Janice: Did you not have insurance love?

Ollie: Don't you worry about a thing love; I'm a painter and decorator by trade. I'll have it right as rain in no-time.

> A paramedic comes on, pops an oxygen mask onto Alice, and leads her off. She reaches back, pulls her mask off, I want Ollie to come with me, I'm going nowhere without him, He saved my bloody life.
>
> Ollie starts to follow, but Colin grabs him.

Colin: You were never a bloody painter and decorator.

Ollie: I know, but I can make it a damn site better than it is right now.

> Ollie exits after Alice.

Janice: Well who'd have thought it, Ollie Dumbar?

ACT TWO SCENE SEVEN— Reconcile. (in chip shop)

Brian: So how long you gonna keep this up

Marge: What?

Brian: The silence.

Marge: I'm not being silent, just don't have anything to say that's all.

Long pause

Brian: Sorry.

Marge glances at Brian and despite wanting to make up, holds her ground.

Brian: I don't want this love, you know I don't

Marge: (exasperated) I know.

They start to attend the chips,

Delivery man enters porting a large box

Delivery Man: Hiya, just need a signature from you.

Brian: whoohoo here it is the twenty first century Margery. We'll be kebab central tonight.

Marge: Bloody hells bells.

Brian: Right Mate, I want it just over here, 'cause I'm moving that fridge and there's a gas pipe already there.

Delivery Man: Oh I don't fit it mate, you need the other guy if you need it fitting, I just deliver.

Brian: Course I need it bloody fitting.

Delivery Man: I ain't got you down for fitting else it would have been the other guy come with it, not me, I'm not insured.

Brian: Surely you know how to do it.

Delivery Man: I do, but I can't, I'm not insured, besides you couldn't put it there anyway.

Brian: eh?

Delivery Man: Where does it get it electricity?

Brian: There! Where the fridge is plugged in.

DeliveryMan shakes he's head and sucks air.

Delivery Man: nah mate, you have to have a terminal outlet fitted now-days, with a separate cut off.

Marge: Bloody told you, everything's half arsed with you.

Brian: So can you get the other bloke to come fit it. How much will that cost?

Delivery Man: Nah mate, that's just what he needs to fit it, he's not insured to fit the pre terminal wiring.

Brian: So who fits that?

Delivery Man: You'd have to get a sparky for that mate.

Brian: Bloody hell, that's gonna cost a fortune.

Delivery Man: That's after your corgi registered gas fitter?

Brian: What?

Delivery Man: And your builder.

Brian: Aye?

Delivery Man: Well you see that gas pipe running down the wall there.

Brian: Yeah

Delivery Man: Well that's exposed that is, you can't have that running over the top of a hot kebab machine else the whole place could go up, has to be behind the wall that does, and tiled!

Brian: Oh for Christ's sake, so what do I need to do?

Delivery Man: you need to get a builder to make a channel to hide that pipe and mains power direct from your box, they you get your Corgi guy to re-route the pipe into the channel, then your sparky to install your terminal box and isolator straight to its own ring. Then your builder to come back and re-tile that area to protect your wires and pipes from the heat, only then my mate can come and plug it in for you. And give you your compliance certificate.

Brian: That's going to cost me a bloody fortune.

Delivery Man: Welcome to the 21st Century. Sign here please mate.

Deliveryman leaves, while Brian sinks in disbelief, Marge begins to laugh quietly to herself at Brian's failures.

Brian: It's not bloody funny

This just makes Marge bust into real laughter.

Brian: (Laughs too) It's not bloody funny.

Marge: Oh Love!.

Brian walks across hugs her head down, their foreheads touch, Brian smiles in lifts her chin up with his forefinger, his expression is that of warmth and sympathy.

Brian: We'll get through.

Marge: Yes.

Brian: We Will.

Marge: I know.

They smile at each other.

Marge: I don't want you to go you know.

Brian: (laughs deeply) I know.

Marge: You Bloody fool.

They embrace and release.

Brian: (sings) Now and then there's a fool such as I am over you

You taught me how to love

And now you say that we are through

I'm a fool, but I'll love you dear

Until the day I die

Now and then there's a fool such as I

Now and then there's a fool such as I

Now and then there's a fool such as I.

ACT TWO SCENE EIGHT— Morley's Close.

If you're lucky, your coin is still up in the air spinning; once it lands your destiny is set that way for life.

So watch yourselves (2beats) you know (beat) as you leave here tonight.

You don't know now, right now any more than I did when I started my shift that night what you're going to be from one minute to the next, hero or villain, heads or tails, killer or victim, dead or alive. It's just two sides of the same bloody coin you know.

But then again it's not just your coin is it? Everyone you know or love has a coin, up there spinning in the air and their coins can fall with even more devastation than your own.

Life. It's like one of those coin drops in the arcade, where one coin starts all the others falling. Lots of falling coins and very few winners.

So, why did I come here, I still don't know. I was telling myself it's for them, for us, for everyone, just for the truth, but the actual truth well if you haven't already guessed, it was for me. You see despite not feeling guilty I still feel I need forgiveness.

And now I'm here, I have 'proper' second thoughts again, they don't need me, coming here, stirring things up after all this time. In their way they've probably moved on and don't give much thought to it, not like me. I still think about it all the time.

 So I thought "bugger it Dave", let sleeping dogs lie, Christ knows they've been through the mill, what am I thinking?

So this is me and here's my train, I've got some digs in Leeds now. Start again. At least I can do that.

And this lot, well set in their ways aren't they. You lot, well, you have the advantage of being sentient to all our ways, our motives and our pains. I can talk to you, can't I, You'll listen to me, You'll just sit and listen, thinking about what I have said... they wouldn't, before I had finished my first sentence they would have already started prattling on about their view or take on things, and nobody gets their point across.

That's what arguments are, a lot of talking and no listening. So what's that make them.. A waste of bloody time.

Well see ya...and take care.

THE END

Description of Cast

Brian
Lead role, (Comedy and tragedy) throughout. Chip shop owner, Elvis fan nearly 50's. Past pleasantly plump.

Marge
Chip Shop wife (Comedy and tragedy) Lead role throughout

late 40's, bold strong woman, pleasantly plump

Ollie:
Typical Male (comedy values) major role. Mid thirties mainly drunk, bit of a lad, speaks/acts before he thinks.

Colin
Modern Male (Romantic interest) major role. Late twenties, slightly more sober than Ollie.

Janice
Barmaid (romantic interest and tragedy) Mid Twenties Barmaid from works at the farmers.

Alice
Seventy Year old Widower.

Craig
Small role incidental, Male Late 40's old flame of Marge, slim attractive.

Mavis
Supporting role, Medium role (comedy) 60+, Dotty Old Bat!

Sal
Supporting Role Medium (Comedy) 50+, slim (well preserved, bit of a flirt)

Carol
Supporting Role Medium (Comedy) 40+, the balance between Sal & Mavis.

Dave Morley
Major role large monologues (Tragedy) (Ex Bouncer 30+)

Mum
Supporting role, Medium role (Comedy & Tragedy) (Janice's Mum) 40-60

Dad
Supporting role, Medium role (Comedy) (Janice's Dad) 40-60

Delivery Man
Incidental

Unnamed Customers x 2
(Any age any sex)

Extras for pub scene & House Fire onlookers.

LEGAL NOTICE

Made in the USA
Middletown, DE
11 October 2017